The Rebirth of Music

by

LA MAR BOSCHMAN

Revival Press
P.O. Box 130
Bedford, Tx.
76021

Seventh printing— March 1987

ISBN Number: 0-938612-04-2

DEDICATION

This book is dedicated to my wife, Teresa. Her long hours of labor, her love and her prayers are an invaluable contribution to our ministry.

CONTENTS

INTRODUCTION

Being involved in a ministry that teaches the importance of lifting up Jesus through music I was excited after reading "The Rebirth of Music." The book is packed with scripture and concepts about music that the church needs.

LaMar shares some very revealing scripture regarding Lucifer's (Satan's) involvement in music before he fell from heaven and his counterfeiting efforts since he has fallen.

Very simply God is the creator of all things and he intends for the church to give light and leadership to the world. We as the body of Christ can no longer allow the world to dictate the trends of music, but we must instead offer music that is unparalleled in power because of the creative power of God that dwells in us.

I highly recommend "The Rebirth of Music" to anyone involved in music ministry or anyone who simply wants to better understand music's role in our lives according to scripture.

Phil Driscoll

PUBLISHER'S FOREWORD

Today, more than ever before, we are seeing the manifestations of Lucifer's dominion. Charging ahead go the shock troops of his army, the myriads of musicians of this day. With lyrics of sensuous deception, rebellion, and the occult; driven into the mind and body by the driving sound of instruments and amplifiers pushed to torturous, earsplitting levels; the message of Lucifer's kingdom goes forth. Thousands give themselves in ecstatic worship before those emissaries of "the god of this age."

God be praised that the One who "sang" the worlds into existence, the true God of all eternity, the One who created music in the beginning, is raising up a pure and shining army to stand against this onslaught. Armed with the two-edged sword of the Word and with the "high praises of God in their mouth," these praising men and women will go forth in the vanguard of the army as did the singers and dancers of Jehoshaphat's day. They will storm the very gates of hell, regain the lost dominion, and stand in the place vacated by Lucifer's fall, leading the angelic hosts in everlasting praise and worship to the Most High God.

As LaMar Boschman shows in this book, such is the breadth and purpose of *The Rebirth of Music*.

THE PUBLISHERS

CHAPTER I

Music in the Beginning

Long before God made man and formed the earth as we know it today, He created an angel in the third heaven and gave him the ability to play music. In fact, he was created with instruments of music built into his very own body. This angel was a special celestial being; he was an archangel. No cherub or seraph was allowed to be closer to the throne of God than he. Only two other angels in heaven equaled his position of authority and responsibility. These were the archangels, Michael and Gabriel.

First was Michael, a warrior and a protector. Second was Gabriel, a messenger. It was Gabriel who told Zachariah and Elizabeth that they were going to bring forth a son who would prepare the way for the Messiah. Gabriel also appeared to Mary saying that she was highly favored among all the women on earth, and that she would bear a son, Jesus, who would be the Saviour of the world. Our musician was the third archangel, and his name was Lucifer.

In Ezekiel the Bible tells us about Lucifer:

The workmanship of thy TABRETS and of thy PIPES was prepared in thee in the day that thou wast created (Ezek. 28:13).

Lucifer had tambourines and pipes built into his body, and had the ability to play these pipes or tambourines extremely

11

well. It is definitely clear that Lucifer excelled in music and that it was part of him. The Bible refers to pipes, plural, meaning there were more than one. And God being who He is, the Creator, probably did not make them all with the same pitch or sound. Since He is creative I like to think He gave them all a distinct and different frequency. The notes were harmonious, blending well with one another. And since there were more than one, possibly three, they could have made a chord, giving a basic structure for melody, or a lead line to be built upon.

Lucifer also had tabrets, or tambourines as part of his makeup, which would give him rhythm, or a beat, to the music that he played. In fact, within Lucifer's makeup represented all the instruments that we know today. The pipes mentioned in Ezekiel 28 were a type of the wind instruments, the tambourines or tabrets represent the percussion instruments. In Isaiah 14:11 it says:

Thy pomp is brought down to the grave, and the noise of thy VIOLS.

Viols are a six stringed musical instrument which represents all stringed instruments. So the total spectrum of instruments that we play today except for electronic instruments were built into Lucifer's body. He could play them all.

Not only was Lucifer a musician, one who could play an instrument, but he was the instrument as well. Lucifer didn't sit down at a piano, he was a piano. And he didn't carry a guitar around his neck, he was a guitar. Lucifer had this talent and a very capable ability to play instruments and to make them sound in worship to God.

Lucifer's name means lightbearer, or day star. He is also called by several other names, like "Son of the Morning" and "the Anointed Cherub." Lucifer was given a definite anointing for serving or ministering in music. In Ezekiel 28:14 and 16 the Bible says that Lucifer dwelt in the mountain of God and was the covering cherub; it was his responsibility to lead all the angelic hosts in praise and worship to God the Father.

He was heaven's choir director. God had created the angels to worship Himself. And Lucifer was to lead them in worship:

> And suddenly there was with the angel a multitude of the heavenly host praising God, and saying, Glory to God in the highest, and on earth peace, good will toward men (Luke 2:13, 14).

> . . . I saw also the Lord sitting upon a throne, high and lifted up, and his train filled the temple. Above it stood the seraphims; . . . . And one cried unto another, and said, Holy, holy, holy, is the Lord of hosts: the whole earth is full of his glory (Isaiah 6:1-3).

> And I beheld, and I heard the voice of many angels round about the throne and the beasts and the elders; and the number of them was ten thousand times ten thousand and thousands of thousands Saying with a loud voice, Worthy is the Lamb that was slain to receive power, and riches, and wisdom, and strength, and honor, and glory, and blessing (Rev. 5:11, 12).

Lucifer's responsibility was to lead the angelic hosts in singing and playing. And he most likely provided the accompaniment on his pipes and tabrets and viols. God had given him a special anointing for this powerful ministry in music. Lucifer was the master musician in heaven. He either was the entire orchestra, or he had a major part in it along with other angels or celestial beings that played instruments. Lucifer would have been the orchestra leader as well as the choir director and master musician.

Music in the beginning was ordained by God and was pleasing to Him. God gave Lucifer the ministry of music for one reason only, and that was to lead the angelic hosts in worship to God. Music was given or created to minister to God the Father. Music was born and birthed in Lucifer to

13

bring worship to the Almighty God. Music in the beginning was created to worship God. Any other use of music other than worship to God is a violation of purpose for which God created music. God did not create music for any secular purpose. He did not even create music for evangelism. God created music for worship. Music can be used to reach the unsaved, but if that is all we use music for we are living beneath our privilege and are not reaching a total spiritual fulfillment in music.

Lucifer was a worship leader. The Bible describes Lucifer as being very wise, and extremely beautiful:

> . . . every precious stone was thy covering, the sardius, topaz, and the diamond, the beryl, the onyx, and the jasper, the sapphire, the emerald, and the carbuncle, and gold (Ezek. 28:13).

Lucifer was an angel of light and radiated with brilliance. Everything about him was perfect from the day he was created.

Then one day in the midst of all the harmony, order and divine music in heaven . . .

> When the morning stars [angels] SANG together, and all the sons of God shouted for joy (Job 38:7)
> . . .

. . . Lucifer sees his own beauty and brilliance and becomes arrogant and lifted up in pride:

> . . . I will ascend into heaven, I will exalt my throne above the stars of God: I will sit also upon the mount of the congregation, in the sides of the north: I will ascend above the heights of the clouds; I will be like the most High (Isa. 14:13-14).

Lucifer began to desire worship for himself. Of course God could not allow this rebellion, and so He kicked Lucifer out of the third heaven and cast him down to the earth. With him went a third of all the angels in heaven because he had tricked them into worshipping him. He desired worship so much, that he conned these angels into bowing and to giving him glory and becoming part of his following:

And there appeared another wonder in heaven . . . Michael and his angels fought against the dragon; and the dragon fought and his angels, And prevailed not; neither was their place found any more in heaven. And the great dragon was cast out, that old serpent, called the Devil, and Satan, which deceiveth the whole world: he was cast out into the earth, and his angels were cast out with him (Rev. 12:3, 7, 8, 9).

. . . I beheld Satan as lightning fall from heaven (Luke 10:18).

By the multitude of thy merchandise they have filled the midst of thee with violence, thou hast sinned: therefore I will cast thee as profane out of the mountain of God: and I will destroy thee, O covering cherub, from the midst of the stones of fire. Thine heart was lifted up because of thy beauty, thou hast corrupted thy wisdom by reason of thy brightness: I will cast thee to the ground, I will lay thee before kings, that they may behold thee (Ezek. 28:16-17).

How art thou fallen from heaven, O Lucifer, son of the morning! How art thou cut down to the ground, which didst weaken the nations! (Isa. 14:12).

Lucifer fell from the lofty position that he once held in the third heaven before the very presence of God. Satan's kingdom now fills the atmosphere around the earth, even to the very surface of the earth. However, the Bible doesn't say that when God cast Lucifer out of His presence that He took away his ministry of music, or his extremely great ability to be wise. The day Lucifer fell, music fell. Music that once was used to worship Almighty God now became music of an earthly nature, it became music of the world and began to appeal to our lower nature instead of appealing to God and our spiritual man (that part of us that has been born of God). Music then, became corrupted. That anointed and powerful ministry of music that Lucifer had in heaven is now corrupted. That ministry is cursed. It now has a false anointing. Lucifer's music is now of the earth, earthly. Lucifer's splendor has been brought down. He fell, as well as his music. He still has that same powerful ministry to create worship but now it is corrupted, and Lucifer uses that ministry to get worship for himself because he craves it. That is why he said:

> . . . I will ascend into heaven, I will exalt my throne above the stars of God . . . I will ascend above the heights of the clouds; I will be like the most High (Isa. 14:13-14).

Lucifer wanted to achieve a higher position, he wanted to be number one, he wanted to be exalted above everything. Lucifer's desire was and is to receive worship for himself.

It is interesting to note the Arab legend that says the first song ever was the lament of Abel.[1] The first secular activity was the murder of Abel and out of that came secular music. The world has always had music connected with their sin. God, however, has always had music connected with worship. MUSIC WAS CREATED BY GOD FOR ONE PURPOSE AND THAT IS TO EXALT THE LORD IN WORSHIP.

---

[1] A lament or a dirge is an expression of extreme grief or sorrow through chanting, wailing or singing. There are many laments in the Old and New Testaments that were sung and accompanied by instruments.

CHAPTER II

Music and Lucifer

Lucifer's association with music is a very profound and definite one. He had the ability to make any sound he wanted to. As we have seen, he not only was a musician, but part of his very being was made up of instruments. In Ezekiel 28:13 and Isaiah 14:11 we see Lucifer had the ability to make music from his very being. These instruments, the viols and tambourines and pipes, were built in him the day he was created and then he fell. Lucifer was the music minister in heaven but he wasn't satisfied. He wanted to be the Pastor. So he rebelled against the divine authority that was placed over him and there was a church split. Any church or group of Christians that goes against the authority God has placed over them has the same mentality and rebellious spirit Lucifer had. Lucifer wanted his own following; his own worshippers. And Lucifer today is still looking for worship. He is still trying to get people to bow down and worship him.

Even in Jesus' day Lucifer was hungry for worship. One day just before Jesus was to enter into His ministry, Satan, who used to be called Lucifer, came to tempt Him. One of the things Satan asked Jesus to do was to fall down at his feet and worship him:

Again, the devil taketh him up into an exceeding high mountain, and sheweth him all the kingdoms of the world, and the glory of them [the glamour and glitter]; And saith unto him, All these things will I give thee, if thou wilt fall down and worship me (Matt. 4:8-9).

Lucifer was saying, "You don't have to go to the cross to set up a kingdom. I'll give all the kingdoms of the world to You right now. You can take a shortcut, Jesus. I'll make You popular. I'll make You Jesus Christ Superstar. Everyone will know You because You will own all these kingdoms." But Jesus said to Satan:

. . . Get thee hence, Satan; for it is written, Thou shalt worship the Lord thy God, and Him only shalt thou serve (Matt. 4:10).

The devil couldn't get Jesus to worship him, but he is still trying to get people to worship him. He is still looking for worshippers.

Today Lucifer is going up to musicians that are potential superstars and offering them the same proposition he offered Jesus. Lucifer is offering the kingdoms of this world and the glory and glamour of them to musicians; if they will get people to worship him. Lucifer is saying, "I'll give you my ability, I'll give you my ministry of music, if you will help me. I will anoint you with my anointing if you will just worship me. I will make you a superstar."

Some of the singers and musicians today have sold their souls so that they can become superstars and have anything they want in the world. These musicians spend days getting high so that their imagination can be free to receive a new song. They want to get in such a frame of mind that they can write a powerful lyric with some great musical accompaniment. The song that comes, or is born, in this manner is purely of the flesh. The inspiration is not from God. It is either from the world, the flesh or the devil. Yet that song becomes a colossal hit and the group is catapulted into super stardom. People flock to their concerts and as soon as they

18

step on the stage tens of thousands of people jump to their feet and begin singing and raising their hands and dancing around. This is a counterfeit of what God is doing in the church today. God is teaching His people to raise their hands in worship and praise and to sing and to clap in joy and rejoicing. But Lucifer has gotten people to sing and dance before him and he uses the groups to receive his worship.

There are many groups that have become superstars and idols in America today that pray to Lucifer before their concerts. Some of the top name groups in the United States give the credit for their ability and their stardom to Lucifer, or Satan. They worship him, they show him homage, and exalt him as a god. There is no doubt that music today gives glory to Lucifer. He has manipulated artists and he has manipulated groups into worshipping him and singing songs about him; giving glory to himself. There are many examples of this today on radio, on television, and on recordings. Lucifer is receiving worship through music.

Have you ever wondered why groups call themselves by such names as "Black Sabbath," and "Grateful Dead"? Why don't they call their groups wholesome names that speak of holiness and cleanliness and things that are right and decent? There is an evilness in the world that requires it to major on evil things. The more evil it is, the more alluring it is. The more evil it is, the more appealing it is. The more fleshly it is, the more it relates to more people. And people desire these things because there is a basic nature in man that is earthly and is attracted to these fleshly, evil ideas and notions. This is very evident in music. Record albums across the country flaunt sex. They exploit evilness. Serpents and satanic influences appear on the record jacket as well as in the recorded product. There are many groups today that give attention and glory to Satan. Nazareth released two albums entitled "Hair of the Dog" and "Expect No Mercy," which featured demon manifestations on the covers. On Savoy Brown's album, "Hellbound Train," are examples of demonic art with pictures of Satan. Satanic and spiritual influence that is there is real and definite. Why is that?

19

Because Lucifer is behind it all. Lucifer has the ability to make music, he has that powerful ministry that is corrupted and evil and you see his influence today more than ever.

A new style of music that began gaining popularity in the 70's and is emerging from the underground is punk rock, sex rock, or new wave. This music is becoming popular to some people because it is sung or played in rebellion. The leaders that have been interviewed from groups that play this style of music say that they do it in pure rebellion to society, to the political system, in rebellion to their parents, and to God. And when the groups come out on stage, they try to be as gross as possible with their bodies, as vulgar as they can with their mouths, and the crowd goes wild. They eat it up. I have seen on television excerpts of live concerts with groups that simulated sexual acts while playing their instruments. In one instance, Mick Jagger was pretending to commit fornication. Artists like Dave Bowie have a style of presentation that is centered around sexual perversion.

There is no doubt that this type of music is appreciated by the devil. Especially when the group or artist actually sings about him in their lyrics. People think that they are worshipping those superstars. Actually they are worshipping Lucifer, the spirit behind them. Frank Zappa once said, "I'm the devil's advocate. We have our own worshippers who are called 'groupies.' Girls will give their bodies to musicians as you would give a sacrifice to a god."

God's Word says:

> . . . I urge you, brothers, in view of God's mercy, to offer your bodies as living sacrifices, holy and pleasing to God—which is your spiritual worship (Rom. 12:1, NIV).

Mick Jagger, lead singer in the Rolling Stones, said, "I deliberately present myself as the personification of the devil."

"Leon Russel preached, sang and boogied with enough spiritual power to make his entire audience stand, jump and dance in frenzied delight." *Empire* magazine after one of his concerts, quoted Russel's manager as saying, "Leon knows he can awake spiritual power in his audience. He knows he has power and enjoys feeling it." My question is who gave him this power?

In Miami, Florida, before 14,000 people the late Jim Morrison (formerly of the Doors) performed with such perversion and indecency that he was arrested and put in jail. The average age of the audience was twelve to fourteen years old. When asked why he did it, he said, "When I'm performing, I'm spiritual."

Many of the great superstars of America and Europe that are idolized by young people around the world are heavily involved in the occult (predominately astrology and demon worship). Their songs speak very clearly of their beliefs and practices. For example, in the "Hotel California" album by the Eagles they sing the song "One of These Nights" describing the singer searching for the devil's daughter, who possesses demons and sexual desires. Bob Larson, in his book *Rock,* points out in the song "Undercover Angel" how well the subtlety by which occult themes are brought out through music. The singer speaks in the song of a "midnight fantasy" to whom he made love in bed. On the surface it seems like simply a bad dream. However, the song is based on the occult phenomenon of succubus, the cohabitation of a human male with a materialized demon spirit that assumes female proportions.

Earth Wind, and Fire before going on stage join hands in a circle to tune in the force of "higher powers." This group has for a long time explored mysticism and some of the members believe that they are incarnations from previous lives.

Meatloaf sings of a "Bat Out of Hell," picturing demons and a mutant biker riding out of the pit of hell. Jim Steinman admits, "I have always been fascinated by the supernatural and always felt rock was the perfect idiom for it." The lead singer of the group says that when he is on stage he "gets possessed."

One of the boldest groups that display evil in their presentations is the Rolling Stones. Record albums entitled "Their Satanic Majesties Request" spell it out pretty clear and plain. Their song "Sympathy for the Devil" has been chosen as an unofficial national anthem for satanists. Another song portraying Satan worship is "Goat's Head Soup," which was recorded at an actual Haitian voodoo ritual. Behind the song you can hear the screams of people becoming possessed with evil spirits. Most people are not aware that the goat's head is the universal symbol of Satan worship, but the Stones are.

Music is a medium for stirring one spiritually. That is why God requires music in our worship to Him. Lucifer will use the same means to stir people to spiritualism. He can create a spiritual atmosphere, and release an evil unction upon the presentation of music, just as God dwells in our praises and the Holy Spirit comes upon us. Music in the world is manipulated by the enemy and is spiritual music, but not of the Holy Spirit.

God has ordained His people to worship Him by singing and praising, and lifting up their hands unto the Lord, even dancing before His name. But the devil is doing the same thing. He is trying to get people to do those same things in worship to him. Why? Because he desires that worship. He desires to copy God's method. Lucifer is not a creator; he is a counterfeit, a copier, a deceiver. Whom are we worshipping in our music? Lucifer is a deceiver and looking for worship just like God is looking for worship. But God is looking for true worshippers who worship Him in spirit and truth (John 4:24). Lucifer was given a powerful ministry of music, to worship within the highest regions of heaven. But today he is fallen. That same ministry he had is now a powerful negative force. The thing that Lucifer can do best is the thing that he was born with and that is music. He did not carry pipes around his neck or a tambourine in his hand. They were built into his body. And as Lucifer is being pressed closer and closer to the earth, and his time is coming nearer and nearer to an end, he is beginning to get nervous. But Lucifer is wise and he has saved his best weapon until last. And that weapon is the thing that he can do best. The thing that he has been doing ever since he was created, and that is playing and directing music. We as God's people are going to see more and more the powerful weapon of music. We haven't yet seen the full potential of what Satan desires to unleash in the world today.

Evil music that is corrupt, wicked, and sensual has been poured out upon the earth in the 1970's. What will be the sound in the 1980's or 1990's if the Lord should tarry that long? I can't imagine any perversion or any music that can be more perverted than that which we have seen and heard today in the cities across North America. And music is getting worse, the dances are getting worse. With the introduction of the disco sound and dance styles came all kinds of sexual exploitations in sight and sound. From the foxy female image and the macho male image to the hard driving rhythms of the music, people could almost fulfill their sexual fantasies on the dance floor when overcome with "Saturday Night Fever." For gays, disco became a good reason to come out of the closet and flaunt their stuff. One rock promoter estimates that 75 percent of all discos are gay operated. The person striving to be a successful businessman opening a new club must of necessity consider the homosexual patronage.

One of the disco dances that is popular is the "Le Freak." It is done by the partners crouching with their knees bent and legs spread and proceed to thrust their pelvises against each other in rhythm to the music. In one disco, two males became jealous as they watched their female partners dance the "Le Freak" with two other males and so they killed them because of the sexual picture it painted in their minds. I think this speaks for itself. Lucifer has taken one more step in perverting our minds. It is no longer normal for people to have normal sexual behaviour in marriage. But it is now considered normal to be gay, and dance the "Le Freak," and show your sexual appetite in a public display on the dance floor.

Satan is slowly brainwashing Americans and Canadians,

and all those who are participating in worship through music and dance around the world. God wants us to be alert to the enemy's craftiness and his sneaky tactics.

> Stand therefore, having your loins girt about with truth . . . (Eph. 6:14).

God wants us to know truth; to be surrounded by truth. God wants the church to be wise to what Satan is doing and to be prepared for battle, for we have not yet seen the full potential that music will have in the world through Satan's influence. And it's through praise and worship, through music to God the Father, that we can have power and victory in our Christian lives.

CHAPTER III

Music — Is It Important?

Music is mentioned in the Bible over 839 times. God must consider music important to mention it that many times in His Word. God doesn't waste words. He doesn't fill in spaces in the Bible. Each word is there for a reason. Hell is mentioned a little over 70 times, yet how much do we know about hell? Most of us can describe it very vividly. We can picture the flames leaping up at us, yet hell is only mentioned 70 times. Music is mentioned 12 times as often. God must consider music very important. In fact, it is one of the major emphases of the Bible.

In Psalm 100:2 it says:

Come before His presence with SINGING.

If I were to appear before the President of the United States I'd be expected to conduct myself in a manner that would show respect. There would be certain manners and courtesies that I would be expected to show, a protocol that would be fitting for the President of the United States. The President of presidents, the King of kings, and the Lord of lords says, "Well, to come into My presence, I want you to come rejoicing with music." Of all the ways God could choose for His people to come into His presence, He chose singing. He didn't say come repenting. He didn't say come into My presence crawling on your knees, screaming confessions. God said, "When

25

you come into My presence, I want you to come singing."
Churches throughout the world are discovering the presence
of God through praise:

> Let us come before Him with thanksgiving and ex-
> tol Him with MUSIC and SONG (Ps. 95:2, NIV).

The Bible says:

> Enter into his gates with thanksgiving (Ps. 100:4).

We sing songs of thankfulness to God telling Him how thank-
ful we are for all He has done for us. Then we enter into His
courts with praise and begin to praise Him verbally, telling
Him how much we love Him. The Bible informs us that God
dwells in the praises of His people. Psalm 22:3 says:

> . . . thou art holy, O thou that inhabitest the prais-
> es of Israel.

We the Church are spiritual Israel (Galatians 6), and God
wants to dwell in our praise: and praise is birthed in music.
David received the greatest revelation of the importance of
music in the house of the Lord. He set priests and Levites
in the house of the Lord whose sole purpose was to provide
music. They were to minister before God with singing and
with instruments of music:

> And these are they whom David set over the SER-
> VICE OF SONG in the house of the Lord, after
> that the ark had rest. And they ministered before
> the dwelling place of the tabernacle of the congre-
> gation with SINGING, until Solomon had built the
> house of the Lord in Jerusalem: and then they
> waited [that means they served] on their office
> according to their order (1 Chron. 6:31-32).

David appointed these priests to look after the service of song or song service. It must have been a very important part of the service in the house of the Lord, because these singers didn't work at any other job. They were on full time staff to minister music in the house of the Lord. They were paid from the tithes of the people and given a place to stay on the church property. They were always available to minister.

> And these are the SINGERS, chief of the fathers of the Levites, who remaining in the chambers were free: for they were employed in that work day and night (1 Chron. 9:33).

> Of the sons of Asaph, the singers were over the business [in other words, the activities] of the house of God. For it was the king's commandment concerning them, that a certain portion should be for the SINGERS, due for every day (Neh. 11: 22-23).

> . . . he had prepared for him a great chamber, where aforetime they laid the meat offerings, the frankincense, and the vessels, and the tithes of the corn, the new wine, and the oil, which was commanded to be given to the Levites, and the SINGERS, and the porters; and the offerings of the priests (Neh. 13:5).

The ministry of music is as important as any other ministry in the house of the Lord. The singers were part of the ministry staff of the church in the Old Testament. They were not only to provide special music, but help lead in worship as well as the song service. The song service is not a mere preliminary, something that we should hurry through so that we can get to the more important part of the service. It's not an ice breaker, it's not something to get people warmed up with. A church service isn't a party. A song service is a prerequisite for the Word. Music prepares us to receive the sermon or the word of the Lord. We should come to minister to (worship) the Lord. That will knit our hearts together in love and bring down the barriers between us and God. Then God can minister to us. The Holy Spirit can flow out and purify us when we come into His presence. Music has the ability to break down barriers, tear down walls, and soften our hearts.

Music prepares us for the Word. In 2 Kings 3 there is an account of Jehoshaphat, king of Judah, and the kings of Israel and Edom wanting help and direction from the Lord. They had journeyed seven days from home and run out of water. They needed water for all their animals and the servants that travelled with them. Having heard that Elisha was a prophet of the Lord, they went to ask him to give them the word of the Lord. The first thing Elisha did was call for a minstrel (a player of a stringed instrument), and ask him to play. Elisha could not prophesy until there was music. After the minstrel had played the "hand" of the Lord came to Elisha and gave him a prophetic utterance, the "word" of the Lord. We see here the importance of music in preparing the way for the word. The first thing Elisha said was, "Bring me a minstrel." The Bible said that when the minstrel played, then the hand of the Lord came upon Elisha, and he spoke very clearly the word of God.

Music is commanded by God to be part of our daily lives as well as part of our worship to Him. The Bible says:

SING unto the Lord, all the earth (Ps. 96:1).

Again:

SING unto the Lord with thanksgiving (Ps. 147:7).

Also:

. . . be filled with the Spirit; Speaking to yourselves in PSALMS and HYMNS AND SPIRITUAL SONGS, SINGING and making MELODY in your heart to the Lord (Eph. 5:18-19).

There are over 200 scriptures that tell us to sing. There are too many to list here, but I think that God is trying to tell us something. Perhaps He likes music. And to Him it is important. That is why He mentions it so much. God loves to hear His bride sing those beautiful love songs that are like a sweet perfume to Him. Those songs of praise that are the fruit of our lips. To God music is important. It has a definite place in worship to the One we love. The ministry of music is a truth that God wants to restore to its fullest potential. The Church has never before in its history flowed in the full capacity that God wants it to in the ministry of music.

Just as we discussed in previous chapters, Lucifer is going to get stronger and stronger in the area of music. And his influence and power with the weapon of music is going to come against the Church. But God is raising up anointed singers and musicians. God considers music important. That's why it is important today that we become part of this plan and become part of the ministry of music. And these a-nointed singers and musicians that God is raising up are going to be sent forth and they are going to go to war. They are going to go into combat against the enemy face to face. And some of that warfare will be through music. The devil trembles at the sound of praises of God's people. When we sing and play the name of Jesus, the enemy is frightened. He is driven back. The ministry of music is a powerful weapon that we can wield against the onslaught of the enemy.

No wonder God considers music important. He wants the Church to be ready and prepared for what is ahead. He's preparing us to make war in the days to come. And these are exciting days we live in. We are seeing God restoring biblical praise and worship to His Church. It excites me to see praise and worship perfected through music and the ministry of music perfected through praise and worship, for the Bible promised a generation that shall be created that shall praise the Lord (Psalm 102:18). I'm glad that I'm a part of that generation to know and understand that music is important to God. Why else would God go to such care and attention to list so many songs in the Bible. The longest book in the Bible is God's songbook—the Book of Psalms. Why? Because

God loves to sing.

> The Lord thy God in the midst of thee is mighty;
> he will save, he will rejoice over thee with joy; he
> will rest in his love, HE will joy over thee with
> SINGING (Zeph. 3:17).

Praise the Lord, God rejoices over us with singing. He must
like music. Jesus proclaims in Hebrews 2:12:

> . . . in the midst of the church will I SING praise
> unto thee [God].

I believe that God the Father, Jesus the Son, and the Holy
Spirit love music because of the place it was given in the Old
and New Testaments. If music is important to God then it
must of necessity be considered important by us.

CHAPTER IV

Music and the Anointing

It is of the utmost importance that music be anointed when we sing and play if it is to minister to people and not just be pretty "special" music. Music in the world is performed to impress or to move others emotionally. Christian music can be impressive and stirring, but if the only reason for using it is to impress people and move their emotions we are doing it with the wrong motive. Something is wrong. God's music goes beyond that. It ministers life and truth because it is presenting and glorifying Jesus. And this can only be done when the musicians, the instruments, the singers, and the songs are anointed (that is, saturated in God's Holy Spirit).

What is the anointing? In the Old Testament, when a king or priest was to take office, he was anointed, that is, oil was poured upon his head (Exodus 29:7) and he was set apart to God. In Exodus 28:41, God told Moses:

> [Take] Aaron thy brother, and his sons with him; and [thou] shalt anoint them, and consecrate them, and sanctify them, that they may minister unto me in the priest's office.

Oil in the Bible is a type of the Holy Spirit. God wants His priests and ministers, which include the singers and musicians, to be anointed. He wants to pour the oil of the Holy

Spirit on every priest ministering in the house of the Lord. Without the presence of the Holy Spirit in our lives and ministry we have nothing to offer except mere words. But when singers and musicians called of God are anointed, and the presence of the Holy Spirit is upon their instruments and voices, great things happen. No wonder in Solomon's temple on dedication day when the singers played, the glory of God so filled the temple that the priests couldn't stand to minister (2 Chronicles 5:12-14). It was because the Levites, who were the singers in verse 12, were anointed and flowing with the Spirit. The anointing of God was upon their music, they were together flowing as a unit. In verse 13 it says:

> It came even to pass, as the TRUMPETERS and SINGERS were as one, to make one sound to be heard in praising and thanking the Lord; and when they LIFTED UP THEIR VOICE with the TRUMPETS and CYMBALS and INSTRUMENTS OF MUSIC, and praised the Lord, saying, For he is good; for his mercy endureth forever: that then the house was filled with a cloud, even the house of the Lord;

The singers and the musicians were as one. They were together making one sound. There was unity among them. They were working together, flowing together in pure praise. So much so,

> . . . that the priests could not stand to minister by reason of the cloud: for the glory of the Lord had filled the house of God (vs. 14).

God dwelt in their praise.

How do we become anointed so that the power of God and the presence of His Holy Spirit will rest upon our music? The answer is simple: through prayer. It is not we who anoint ourselves. It is Jesus who pours the oil and the Holy Spirit on those who want it. We must ask Him to anoint us

32

every time we are going to sing, every time we are going to play an instrument, and even when we are asked to lead songs in worship. We must ask God to anoint us and guide us by His Spirit to know what songs to play, and what songs to sing, that every song we play and sing will be saturated and filled with oil of the Holy Spirit. Only then can we minister to those who hear our music.

Too many song leaders in churches today when leading in worship, pick favorites or popular choruses or songs, instead of asking God what He would like for His people to sing. There is nothing wrong with singing popular or favorite choruses, but let's not ask each other what's our favorite, or ask for favorites from the pulpit, but let's ask God before the service what songs He wants us to sing. God has a purpose and a desire for every service. We don't just gather for the sake of having a church service; that's ritual, and it becomes religion. We gather to worship the King of kings and the Lord of lords and to receive and to respond to what God wants to say to us in the service. We should seek the mind of the Lord when we enter a service to know what God wants to accomplish in a particular service. Just as much as the minister who is to preach the Word studies and prays and asks God what he should preach, so the song leader should ask God what songs he should use to lead the people in worship.

Without the anointing covering every part of the vessel, the flesh will show. The oil of the Holy Spirit must cover us from the head to the toes, including our instrument. It is my prayer that this vessel would be so saturated in the anointing oil that no flesh shall ever glory in the presence of the Lord.

It is very important as a musician, singer, song leader, choir, or orchestra leader to learn to flow under the anointing. It is difficult when a service is choppy and the songs jump from one topic to another with no theme, to try and know exactly what God is saying in the meeting. When it is all over, can you tell precisely what God is trying to say to us? When a good service is over you know exactly what God has said because from beginning to end there has been a theme or flow that has been woven like a thread throughout every part of the service, tying it all together. This common theme keeps the service from being disjointed or chopped up.

A flow in a service comes by everyone: the pastor, the song leader, the choir director, the orchestra leader, the singers, the musicians, and the congregation praying and seeking God for the mind of the Lord for that service. When God gives a thought, an idea, a song or a word, stay on that theme unless the Holy Spirit directs you or quickens down another line. When everyone has done their part in finding out what God wants to accomplish in the meeting, you will probably discover that what the choir sang and what the pastor preached were the same thoughts. Often the songs sung in worship bring the glory and the conviction of the Holy Spirit upon the people in such a way that the altar call is taken before the sermon is ever preached. Why does this happen? Because we let God have His way. There is a theme and a purpose all the way through. The anointing and flow in a service are absolutely essential if we want God to use the service to its maximum potential. Without the anointing and flow the meeting is disjointed and lifeless. But with the anointing on the musicians, the singers, and everyone else who has a part in the service, the presence of God can be brought into the service. Just as in King Solomon's temple, you can expect great things to happen.

If we are together, in one accord, lifting up our voice with one sound to worship and praise the Lord, there is unity. Unity comes only through prayer, through flowing together, and in trying to minister according to what God's desire and will is for a particular service. God help us as singers and musicians never to get up and play not having prayed and asked God to anoint our instrument, our singing and our songs; because if we do, our singing and our playing will be just pretty music. It will not be used to the maximum potential. God wants us to be anointed when we sing and minister in music. It is not talent that breaks the yoke over people's lives and sets the captive free. It is not your great musical ability that brings God's glorious power. The Word of God says it is the anointing that breaks the yoke. The anointing is absolutely essential if our music is to minister.

Not by might, nor by power, but by my spirit saith the Lord of hosts (Zechariah 4:6).

CHAPTER V

Music and the Prophetic

In the Word of God there is a close association between music and prophecy. In the story from the book of Chronicles, when King Jehoshaphat of Judah was seeking direction from God regarding victory over the armies of Ammon, Moab and Mt. Seir, it was through a musician which God spoke that direction. There was a prophetic mantle on him as he worshipped the Lord. Throughout the Bible there is a close relationship between music and the prophetic.

Many of the Psalms are considered to be prophetic. And that book is a collection of songs written during a long period of time extending from the time of Moses to the post-exile era of the second temple. Seventy-three songs in the book were written by David, twelve by Asaph, ten by the sons of Korah, two by Solomon; and Moses, Heman and Ethan each wrote one. These songs were recorded as part of Holy Scripture because of the prophetic content in them. For example, prophecies about the coming Messiah being fulfilled in Jesus Christ were numerous:

PROPHETIC SONG	SUBJECT	SONG FULFILLED
Psalm 2:7	Declared the Son of God	Matthew 3:17
Psalm 110:4	To be a priest	Hebrews 5:5, 6
Psalm 41:9	Betrayed by a friend	Luke 22:47, 48
Psalm 35:11	Accused by false witness	Mark 14:57, 58

PROPHETIC SONG	SUBJECT	SONG FULFILLED
Psalm 35:19	Hated without reason	John 14:24, 25
Psalm 22:7, 8	Scorned and mocked	Luke 23:35
Psalm 69:21	Given vinegar and gall	Matthew 27:34
Psalm 109:4	Prayer for His enemies	Luke 23:34
Psalm 22:17, 18	Soldiers gambled for His coat	Matthew 27:35, 36
Psalm 34:20	No bones broken	John 19:32, 33, 36
Psalm 16:10	To be resurrected	Mark 16:6, 7
Psalm 49:15	To be resurrected	Mark 16:6, 7
Psalm 68:18	His ascension to God's right hand	1 Cor. 15:4, Eph. 4:8

King David and the others who sang those songs were moved upon and used of the Holy Ghost.

The same prophetic mantle that was upon these biblical songwriters can be upon musicians and songwriters today. I have heard in churches across the continent musicians and singers singing songs of prophecy. God in His grace has seen fit to give me a song of prophecy entitled "Sons and Daughters." What a joy when you feel that prophetic anointing come upon you. Prophetic songs do not have to come only in the form of a song, as such, with three verses and a chorus. They can also come as scripture songs or choruses. They can be of any length. One of the most powerful anthems of praise that I have heard came forth with a prophetic anointing in the midst of a congregation is the song, "All Hail, King Jesus." It will lift you into realms of worship that are exhilarating.

David being a musician himself knew the place the ministry of music should have in the house of the Lord. He set aside whole families to be musicians before the Ark. Their job was to prophesy on those instruments.

Moreover David and the captains of the host

separated to the service of the sons of Asaph, and of Heman, and of Jeduthun, who should prophesy with HARPS, with PSALTERIES, and with CYMBALS (1 Chron. 25:1).

These musicians did not only accompany the choir or congregational singing. They were part of the prophetic ministry in the church. They *prophesied* on their instruments. The instrument as well as the musician ministered the prophetic.

... under the hands of their father Jeduthun, who prophesied with a HARP, to give thanks and to praise the Lord (1 Chron. 25:3).

The total number of musicians that David appointed to prophesy with instruments of music was 288 (1 Chronicles 25:7).

There are several accounts in the Word of God connecting music with prophecy. In the book of Samuel the story is related how Samuel anointed Saul and kissed him and then told Saul what was going to happen to him after he left:

As you approach the town, you will meet a procession of prophets, coming down from the high place with LYRES, TAMBOURINES, FLUTES and HARPS being played before them, and they will be prophesying. The Spirit of the Lord will come upon you in power and you will prophesy with them; and you will be changed into a different person (1 Sam. 10:5, 6, NIV).

This group of prophets Saul met had instruments of music with them. If they indeed were prophets who spoke the prophetic word of God as the Holy Spirit moved upon them, why did they have musical instruments? Because music prepares the heart to receive the word of the Lord. The worship and praise to God on the instruments brought down the presence of God. It also prepared their hearts to receive the word and prepared the hearts of the listeners to accept the word of the Lord.

There was another prophet in the Old Testament that had music played before he prophesied:

> But now bring me a MINSTREL. And it came to pass, when the MINSTREL played, that the hand of the Lord came upon him [Elisha]. And he said, Thus saith the Lord . . . (2 Kings 3:15, 16a).

Elisha also knew the importance music has in receiving and flowing in the anointing. The minstrel played and the music created an atmosphere of worship and praise in which God could dwell. God dwells in the praises of His people (Psalm 22:3). What makes the ministry of music so powerful is when God not only dwells in our music, but through our music speaks a prophetic word.

It is my desire to see more Christian musicians flow in the prophetic. There are literally thousands of gospel music groups using music purely for evangelism. Praise the Lord for those that are hearing the gospel through music; but what about the millions of Christians that need to hear the prophetic word of God? Who need direction, comfort, and edification in their lives. God wants to use musicians as vessels to speak through. The ministry of music is more than just reaching the unsaved. God wants musicians to prophesy on their instruments, and to play a new song, a spontaneous song of praise and worship, completely unrehearsed. This requires musicians to be free in their worship to allow the Holy Spirit to move upon them. We must give Him time in the service and room in our ministry to accomplish His will.

> Wherefore, brethren, covet to prophesy (1 Cor. 14:39).

CHAPTER VI

Music in Warfare

Another area music is associated with is war. On the surface this seems absurd, but think about the films you've seen of armies, marching in perfect cadence to the martial sound of bugle and drum. Music will lift your emotions and spirit and, in turn, make your faith stronger. Perhaps that is why armies in history, even in the Bible, have gone to war singing.

Today God is gathering together an army which, empowered by the Holy Spirit, captained by Jesus himself, will be the most powerful force that has ever moved across the face of the earth. God is commanding every soldier to:

> Put on the whole armour of God, that ye may be able to stand against the wiles of the devil. For we wrestle not against flesh and blood, but against principalities, against powers, against the rulers of the darkness of this world, against spiritual wickedness in high places (Eph. 6:11, 12).

This army is the Church, His Bride, which is going to war against the enemy and defeat him.

The army of the Lord is going to be a musical army. An army that loves to sing and play instruments. God has commanded His people to:

41

Let the high praises of God be in their mouth, and
a twoedged sword in their hand (Ps. 149:6).

He wants His army not only to be equipped with swords
but with praises. Note: these praises are not just ordinary
praises (if praises can be ordinary), but these are "high
praises." Praises that come out of our mouth with volume
and with authority.

What is this army going to do with these swords and
high praises? The Bible says they are going:

To execute vengeance upon the heathen, and pun-
ishments upon the people; To bind their kings with
chains, and their nobles with fetters of iron; To
execute upon them the judgment written: this
honour have all his saints (Ps. 149:7-9).

God is going to war with an army of worshippers; those who
know how to praise loudly.

Joshua commanded an army that knew how to sing,
shout, and play instruments with volume. In Joshua 6 God
was very specific about how He wanted this army to defeat
the city of Jericho. Their one and only weapon was music
and the shout of victory.

Then the Lord said to Joshua . . . March around
the city once with all the armed men. Do this for
six days. Have seven priests carry TRUMPETS OF
RAM'S HORNS in front of the ark. On the seventh
day, march around the city seven times, with the
priests blowing the TRUMPETS. When you hear
them sound a long blast on the TRUMPETS, have
all the people give a loud shout; then the wall of
the city will collapse and the people will go up,
every man straight in (Josh. 6:2a, 3-5, NIV).

Joshua and his army did exactly what God commanded them
to do. They picked up the ark of the covenant and put it on

their shoulders. Seven priests positioned themselves in front of the ark with trumpets in their hands. In front of the priests, as well as behind the ark of the covenant, went a company of armed guards.

When Joshua gave the order to advance, the mighty processional began. With the trumpets sounding the army marched around the city:

> The armed guard marched ahead of the priests who blew TRUMPETS, and the rear guard followed the ark. All this time the TRUMPETS were sounding (Josh. 6:9, NIV).

Joshua led his army around the city of Jericho once each day for six days. On the seventh day, they did as God told Joshua and marched around the city seven times all the while playing instruments. The Bible then says:

> The seventh time around, when the priests sounded the TRUMPET blast, Joshua commanded the people, "SHOUT, for the Lord has given you the city" . . . When the TRUMPETS sounded, the people shouted and at the sound of the TRUMPET when the people gave a loud shout, the wall collapsed; so every man charged straight in, and they took the city (Josh. 6:16, 20, NIV).

These Old Testament accounts are not just stories for our reading pleasure. They are for our instruction and example (1 Corinthians 10:11). God is instructing us, as a last day generation, to prepare ourselves for confrontation with the enemy. He said nation will fight against nation and kingdom against kingdom and then you will be handed over to be persecuted and put to death and you shall be hated by every nation. But in the midst of this turmoil God is still in control and leading His army and they will know no defeat. For in the midst of this army are musicians playing instruments with authority; there are singers with high praises of God in their mouth. The entire host is marching in strength and victory, rejoicing in their God and no one can stop them. With the songs of worship resounding in volume, the gates of hell cannot stand against this army. The walls have to collapse at the shout of victory for God is the Captain of this mighty host.

There was another army in the Bible that was very musical. They too learned the secret of going to war with instruments of music. One day in the house of the Lord, as all of Judah was standing before the Lord asking for deliverance from the three armies that were come to destroy them, the Holy Spirit came upon one of the musicians. His name was Jahaziel. He was a fifth generation to Asaph, who was one of the chief musicians in David's tabernacle. Jahaziel began to prophesy:

> Listen, King Jehoshaphat and all who live in Judah and Jerusalem! . . . do not be afraid or discouraged because of this vast army, for the battle is not yours but God's . . . you will not have to fight this battle . . . go out to face them tomorrow and the Lord will be with you (2 Chron. 20:15, 17, NIV).

When all of Judah heard the word of God they fell before the Lord and worshipped Him. Then they stood and praised the Lord with a loud voice.

In the morning the people of Judah arose early and prepared themselves to go out and face the enemy. Jehoshaphat knew the secret and the power of the ministry of music in praise, so he appointed singers "unto the Lord" (vs. 21). These singers were not the nation's superstars. They were not a club group recruited from the nearest Holiday Inn. They were singers that had a heart to worship God and lived a pure life before the Lord. They were appointed unto the Lord; not unto Jehoshaphat; not unto the people to entertain them but unto the Lord to praise Him in the beauty of holiness.

The singers went out in front of the army. I can see it now—the sopranos went first, then the altos, the tenors and

44

last the basses. Who knows, maybe the orchestra followed the choir. However, lastly came the army, mighty men of God and in front of them were the more delicate musicians.

> . . . when they began to SING and to praise, the Lord set ambushments against the children of Ammon, Moab and Mount Seir, which were come against Judah; and they were smitten (2 Chron. 20:22).

The enemy had heard the sound of their praises. It rolled across the landscape as claps of thunder and the enemy became frightened. Judah was not even in view yet, but their music could be heard. It was when they started to sing and praise that the Lord set ambushments against the three armies that were out to destroy them.

There are many musicians that sing, but fewer that praise the Lord when they sing. The Bible doesn't say when they sang and entertained the people that God set ambushments against the enemy; it says when they praised, God's power was unleashed. This is the secret to the powerful ministry of music—the singers and musicians are appointed UNTO THE LORD to PRAISE HIM in the beauty of holiness. God is challenging us as Christian musicians to be praisers with our music:

> The men of Ammon and Moab rose up against the men from Mt. Seir [when they heard Judah's praises] to destroy and annihilate them. After they finished slaughtering the men from Mt. Seir, they helped to destroy one another (2 Chron. 20:23, NIV).

I wonder whom the Lord used to ambush the enemy? Judah wasn't there yet. Do you suppose God sent a legion of angels to confuse the army of Ammon, Moab and Mt. Seir? Perhaps an angel picked up a sword and stabbed a man from Ammon through the heart. A friend of his saw it and thought the Moabite soldier standing nearby did it, and avenged his friend's death. And the rest is not hard to imagine. No one saw the angels, while three armies were ambushed. Meanwhile the choir was still marching forward singing, "Praise the Lord for His mercy endureth forever and ever," not knowing what was happening on the other side of the hill:

> When the men of Judah came to the place that overlooks the desert and toward the vast army, they saw only dead bodies lying on the ground, no one escaped. So Jehoshaphat and his men went to carry off their plunder and they found among them a great amount of equipment and clothing and also articles of value—more than they could take away. There was so much plunder that it took three days to collect it. On the fourth day they assembled in the Valley of Beracah, where they praised the Lord. This is why it is called the Valley of Beracah to this day.
> Then, led by Jehoshaphat, all the men of Judah and Jerusalem returned joyfully to Jerusalem, for the Lord had given them cause to rejoice over their enemies, they entered Jerusalem and went to the Temple of the Lord with HARPS and LUTES and TRUMPETS (2 Chron. 20:24-28, NIV).

There are a lot of "secrets" in this story that can teach us many things. For example, these musicians and singers knew the secret of praising the Lord with their music in the valley and on the mountain top. They worshipped on their instruments when surrounded by the enemy and it seemed everything was against them. When the victory came, they did not forget where it came from and returned to the temple to bless the Lord with their harps, lutes and trumpets.

God is raising up strong and powerful ministries of music in churches around the world. He is preparing them to be leaders in warfare against the enemy. The anointed singers and musicians are going to go to battle against the enemy just as King Jehoshaphat did.

CHAPTER VII

The Healing Power of Music

Did you know that music can relieve nerve tension and restore a mind when it is fatigued? That it can bring joy and peace to a heart that is upset and troubled? That music can even reverse sickness and bring healing? Music, even in the natural, can be used in a positive way to restore. If it can restore physical health, think of what it can do to restore our spiritual health. Music has the power and ability to set our minds and spirits free.

The medical staff at the Veteran's Hospital in Lyons, New Jersey, conducted a project in music therapy and found it to be a great success in the treatment of nervous and mental disorders. Other hospitals have found music to be effective in the curing of arthritis, spastic-paralysis and the restoring of heart fatigue. Music relaxes and soothes people who are disturbed in their minds and tend to brood. It gives them some balance.

Amnesia can be treated well through music. It will bring back forgotten memory associations more quickly than any other means. The patient is able to recall names, ideas, places and people, by listening to music. A song will trigger an idea, a color or sound, or picture and those things that were lost in the past will be brought back to the patient's remembrance.

Music can free us from tension and lift our spirits when we are discouraged. It can literally move our emotions and then our will. Have you ever been upset and angry and determined to do something a certain way when you get home? As you are driving along the music on the FM dial of the radio begins to relax you. You begin to re-think the situation and before you're home you've changed your mind because you see your attitude has been too harsh.

Have you ever been driving in bumper to bumper traffic and noticed that your frustrations were either increasing or diminishing, depending on which radio station you were listening to? Obviously there is an effect from the music you are listening to. Music can move your emotions which, in turn, will move you. That is why music is such a powerful tool.

Music is used in advertising to make you feel like a certain product will change your life. Sociologists say that music is a vehicle for communicating, influencing and controlling our spirit, mind and body. A song will present a thought and if you listen to that song enough times it will permeate your total being. That is what educated professors say about how commanding the vehicle music is. It can be a powerful source for achieving a positive or negative goal.

King Saul was once bothered by an evil spirit that God allowed to come upon him. Saul probably received very bad headaches and became sick physically and mentally. There were times when Saul became very depressed and afraid:

> But the Spirit of the Lord departed from Saul, and an evil spirit from the Lord troubled him. And Saul's servants said unto him, Behold now, an evil spirit from God troubleth thee. Let our lord now command thy servants, which are before thee, to seek out a man, who is a CUNNING PLAYER on an HARP: and it shall come to pass, when the evil spirit from God is upon thee, that he shall PLAY with his hand, and thou shalt be well (1 Sam. 16: 14-16).

Somehow King Saul's servants knew the powerful

remedy music can be. Perhaps they knew from past experience, or perhaps that knowledge had been passed down to them from generation to generation.

It was not good enough for the servants to call any harp player. The suggestion to the king by the servants was to look hard for a cunning or a very skillful player:

> And Saul said unto his servants, Provide me now a man that can PLAY well, and bring him to me (1 Sam. 16:17).

One of the servants spoke up and told King Saul that he had seen one of the sons of Jesse, the Bethlehemite, who was not only a very talented musician but good looking, brave, strong, and had a good head on his shoulders (good solid judgment). Everyone knew that the Lord was with David. Saul took the suggestion from his servant and sent a messenger to bring this lad to him. The boy's name was David.

Jesse was pleased that the king wanted to see his son so he sent David with an ass loaded with bread, wine and a young goat. When Saul saw David he immediately liked him and asked David to be his armour bearer and body guard. David was always near Saul so when the evil spirit bothered Saul, David could play his harp and the music would soothe the king.

> And it came to pass, when the evil spirit from God was upon Saul, that David took AN HARP, and PLAYED with his hand: so Saul was refreshed, and was well, and the evil spirit departed from him (1 Sam. 16:23).

Note here that it was purely on the presentation of an anointed song by a skillful musician that Saul was delivered from the evil spirit. No doctor treated him. It was not a tranquilizer that subdued the disturbing influence of the evil spirit. It was the delivering power of God that was on the harp David played that set Saul free. David didn't sing a word. The anointing was on the instrument and the music that came forth broke the bands that had King Saul tied to the evil spirit.

> And it shall come to pass in that day, that his burden shall be taken away from off thy shoulder, and his yoke from off thy neck, and the yoke shall be destroyed *because of the anointing* (Isa. 10:27).

It was the music, and the anointing upon the musician and the instrument, that broke the yoke of bondage for King Saul.

Music is good medicine, and it can bring healing; however, at the same time it can bring sickness upon us, depending on what form we listen to. Performers of loud music can suffer from ulcers, insomnia and heart trouble. Due to increased volume and the type of music played, it can bring intense pain to the body of the performer and audience. Music always affects the body. It is a powerful instrument. Music can hypnotize; it can put you to sleep, it can make you hyper. It has been proven that certain sound waves, low enough in frequency, can even kill you. These waves lie within the range below your hearing (infasonics). Even at seven cycles per second, sound can cause considerable pain and has the potential to kill people, en masse, up to five miles away. Music can be a tremendous destructive force or a tremendous healing force.

No wonder God commanded us to SING praises to Him in the *beauty* of holiness. He knew those sweet notes of harmony would bring health to His people. Let us as musicians and singers be responsible with our music and minister to people in healing. Let us bring peace and deliverance through music played in the name of the Lord.

CHAPTER VIII

Which Music Is of God?

There has been much controversy in the past decade about music in Christian circles and about certain instruments in the church. When I was fourteen and was learning to play the guitar, a church in the town that I lived in had a hard time accepting the guitar as an instrument that can be played in the house of the Lord. After a while the church realized that guitars were popular with the young people. So in their youth meetings they allowed acoustic guitars to be played in the sanctuary, but no electric guitars and amplifiers were allowed in the church services. It is interesting to note that today, in those same churches, you will find amplifiers on the platform. Did God change His mind? Was it once wrong to use certain instruments in church in our worship and now is it okay? Or did man make up those restrictions? I think the answer is quite obvious. God commanded His people thousands and thousands of years ago to:

> Praise the Lord with the HARP: make music to Him on the TEN STRINGED LYRE. Sing to Him a new song; PLAY skillfully and shout for joy (Ps. 33:2, 3, NIV).

> Sing for joy to God our strength; shout aloud to the God of Jacob! Begin MUSIC, strike the TAMBOURINE, play the melodious HARP and LYRE.

Sound the RAMS HORN [trumpet] at the new moon . . . (Ps. 81:1-3, NIV).

And of Zion it shall be said . . . as well the singers as the PLAYERS on INSTRUMENTS shall be there . . . (Ps. 87:5a, 7a).

It is clear that God has ordained in Zion, His Church, that He wants instruments as well as singers to blend together to worship His name. Even today there are some people who find it hard to accept certain instruments that can be used to worship God. God is doing a whole new thing in the ministry of music in His Church. Churches all over the world are using all kinds of instruments to worship the Lord. And these churches are discovering that the joy of the Lord can be found in God's house. They are finding liberty in their worship. Man has said, "Guitars and drums are of the devil," but God has said that we are to:

Praise him with the sound of the TRUMPET: praise him with the PSALTERY and HARP. Praise him with the TIMBREL [that is, a tambourine] and dance: praise him with STRINGED INSTRUMENTS and ORGANS. Praise him upon the LOUD CYMBALS; praise him upon the high sounding CYMBALS (Ps. 150:3-5).

These are all instruments known in David's time, but just to make sure that we don't exclude any other instruments in our worship:

Let everything that hath breath praise the Lord (Ps. 150:6a).

God does not want us to get hung up on the instruments. The important thing is that we praise Him. That is why Psalm 150 ends with a command of the Lord:

PRAISE YE THE LORD.

If we love Him we will praise Him the way He wants us to. It's a command. We don't do it just because we feel like it, but because God commands His people to praise Him.

Not only has there been much controversy over certain types of instruments as to whether or not they are totally of the world and have no place in the church, there has also been much discussion over certain styles of music. Do certain types of music have a place in the body of Christ?

All instruments and music came from God originally. This is confirmed by the fact that it was God who put the tambourines, pipes, and viols in Lucifer when he was created in the first place. It was God that inspired David to invent and make instruments.

We cannot limit God. However, I've noticed that the closer musicians get to being like the world, the more flesh can be seen in their presentations, rather than the sincere Spirit of God.

Groups that idolize the music of the world, and try to copy other groups in the world, are in a very dangerous situation. God wants His ministers of music to have more to offer than just salvation. We aren't to be so much like the world that the world can't see any difference in us. If we dress like the world and act like the world, we will be seen to be just like the world. But we are to be "set apart from the world."

God has enlarged our vision. He wants us to have more to offer people than just a few fancy guitar licks and some funky harmonies in piano solos. He wants us to be able to offer salvation and the truths of the Holy Spirit. God wants us to be able to share these with others, and it must come out in our *music*. We shouldn't dress sloppy on the platform. We shouldn't act real "cool and hip." We are to let the people see Jesus in us. If they don't see Jesus, then there is too much flesh; there is too much of us. We must decrease, but God must increase.

God is enlarging the spectrum of Christian music that is available today. Because of that we don't need the world's music anymore. God is causing there to be a division between the SONG OF THE LORD and the SONG OF THE WORLD.

Songs of the world fit into one of three categories: they are either of the WORLD, the FLESH or the DEVIL. Songs of the WORLD may just be pretty love songs; about a wife, a puppy or a beautiful sunset. There is nothing necessarily wrong with these songs; they may be beautiful and express love and admiration for a person or object on a natural level.

Songs of the FLESH are generally lusty songs that are sensual and dirty. They are sexual; the thoughts of these songs present ideas that appeal to us sexually. They are smutty and only serve to edify the flesh.

Songs of the DEVIL are directly anointed of Satan. These songs are evil. They present thoughts of blasphemy, and are songs that exalt Lucifer or Satan as the supreme being.

There are thousands of songs that fit into these three categories, and they are all songs of the world, the flesh or the devil. It is surprising how many Christians that wouldn't watch a smutty scene on television or go to a restricted movie will listen continually to worldly music. Without realizing it they are feeding their minds with dirty and suggestive thoughts. All they are doing is satisfying their flesh. The Bible says crucify the deeds of the flesh. The more we listen to music that talks about getting high on dope or about leaving your wife for another woman, the more we are feeding our minds with thoughts that are directly in conflict with God's Word.

Lyrics of many of today's songs say "if it feels good do it." But God says that if it is right, do it. If there is any doubt, stay away from it. Yet as Christians we are feeding our minds with this garbage that is lusty and greedy. We wonder why we have such a struggle serving the Lord. Are we listening to the world's music more than we are listening to God's music? I sincerely hope we are not.

As Christians we should be feeding our minds with wholesome songs. Songs that tell of victory and faith; songs of power, songs of love and songs of grace, joy and peace. The Bible says:

. . . whatsoever things are true, whatsoever things are honest, whatsoever things are just, whatsoever things are pure, whatsoever things are lovely, whatsoever things are of good report; if there be any virtue, and if there be any praise, think on these things (Phil. 4:8).

We should not feed ourselves with the garbage of the world but the things that are pure, the things that are honest, the things that are true, the things that are just, and things that are lovely and of good report. These things are what we're to think about. These things we are to sing about. These things are what we are to listen to.

Look what happens when you take out of that verse the word "things" and substitute the word "songs":

. . . whatsoever songs are true, whatsoever songs are honest, whatsoever songs are just, whatsoever songs are pure, whatsoever songs are lovely, whatsoever songs are of good report; if there be any virtue, and if there be any praise, sing these songs (or, think on these songs!).

God has made it possible that today we don't need the world's music any more. The Church has music that exalts and magnifies the Lord.

Music in the world has become so perverted that God is causing there to be a division between songs that are sexually explicit (with sexually explicit lyrics that range from homosexuality to Satan worship), and songs that exalt the Lord and edify the believer. Now that is a good definition of God's music: Songs that exalt the Lord and edify the believer.

Sociologists in secular circles have proven that music is extremely powerful. First it communicates an idea or thought. Then it influences our view of that idea. Lastly it controls our mind, soul and spirit. Think of the power that is available to Lucifer and what he can do with music in the negative. Then consider what potential music can have with a positive building up of the body of Jesus Christ and the Kingdom of God.

If music in the world could eventually control our mind then it is a serious thing to consider what kind of music we listen to. There may be nothing wrong with a love song about a girl, but songs that are dirty, and magnify Lucifer have no place in the life of a born again Christian. God wants there to be a definite line drawn in the area of music. He wants us to clean up our act in the area of music. The Bible says:

> Love not the world, neither the things that are in the world. If any man love the world, the love of the Father is not in him. For all that is in the world, the lust of the flesh, and the lust of the eyes, and the pride of life, is not of the Father, but is of the world. And the world passeth away, and the lust thereof: but he that doeth the will of God abideth forever (1 John 2:15-17).

The Bible further says:

> Let the word of Christ dwell in you richly in all wisdom (Col. 3:16a).

Are you into the Word as much as you are into your music? We are to teach the Word to others through

> . . . psalms and hymns and spiritual songs, singing with grace in your hearts to the Lord (Col. 3:16b).

You and I are called to be priests or teachers of the Word. So our songs should have a lot of Bible content. This music is of God.

It is very clear that God doesn't want us to be involved with the music of the world. God wants us to draw the line. He wants us to listen to music that is wholesome, good, and pure. Christian musician, do you love the music of the world?

Do you try to copy and play like the musicians in the world? God says, "If any man love the world, the love of the Father is not in HIM." Those are heavy words. He wants us to play songs that are wholesome, that are clean, that edify the believer, or exalt Jesus as Lord, that the people of the world can clearly see Jesus in.

Songs that have a double meaning, that can be taken either way, the world does not see Jesus in. They do not take a song about love that has no mention of God and automatically think about Jesus when you sing a lyric like "I love the touch of your tender hands." The worldly person will begin to think you are singing about something that has sexual connotations. They will not assume you are singing about God even if they know you are a Christian. We must be careful what we feed other people's minds. The world is still asking the questions, "Well, who are you talking about? What's it all about? I don't understand."

Remember, God wants us to sing and play music that will exalt Jesus as Lord, songs that are pure and that will edify the believer. Which music is of God? Which music is of the world? It should be very clear if you will just ask the question, "Who, or what, does it exalt?" Is the answer, "The world, the flesh, or the devil?" Music of God is music that exalts Jesus and edifies the believer. Think on the things that are pure, and listen to that music which is wholesome, and you will be a happier, more victorious Christian.

CHAPTER IX

Music — A Sign of Restoration and Revival

Joyful music in the church has always been a sign of restoration and revival. Restoration is the bringing back or re-establishing of something as it once was. This is also what revival is—reviving or returning to a former state. What died will be made alive again. What was lost shall be found. Revival is not a week of meetings—it is a rebirth.

Music has always been associated with revival. In church history, with every restoration of doctrinal truth, there has been a restoration in the ministry of music. With every new revelation of scripture, there has been a fresh revelation in the music in the Church. Why? Because music is an outward response of an inward rebirth.

The Reformation period clearly bears this out. With the increase in the knowledge and revelation of God's Word, there came forth a new song. During the dark ages, when all clear understanding of scripture was lost, there was no music in the church. Only the religious hierarchy were allowed to chant their prayers. The common people were not allowed to sing in the church. When Martin Luther received the revelation of the meaning of the scripture;. . . the just shall live by faith (Rom. 1:17), there sprang up a spiritual rebirth in the church. For the first time men understood they could be saved through faith in the Son of God. In the revival that followed there came out of the church a new sound. The Church began to sing songs again for the first time since the early church. Luther began to write songs that were contemporary with the latest chords and rhythms, songs that even the common people could sing in worship to God.

And so it was with every truth that was restored to the Church, there was a restoration in music. Even at the turn of the century when the Holy Spirit was poured out in California, there was a new sound in the Church. People began to sing praises. There was a rebirth in the ministry of music as well. Then, in the early 1950's, with the restoration of the truth of the five-fold ministries: apostle, prophet, evangelist, pastor and teacher, and the restoration of the laying on of hands, there was once again new music in the Church. Christians began to sing scripture songs. They began to sing songs in the Spirit for the first time. While worshipping the Lord out loud, while singing praises to His name, many would sing out a new song that they had never sung before. This new song would edify and comfort the Body. Many of the songs we sing in our ministry have been received this way.

Praise the Lord that He has also restored these types of music to the Church:

Psalms—scriptures set to music
Hymns—anthems of the Church
Spiritual songs—songs received, sung and quickened
    by the Holy Spirit

A new joy in the music of the Church is a result of spiritual renewal.

In the Old Testament there were many revivals of truth in which music was a part. In the revival under Nehemiah, music was present. One of the first things that Nehemiah did after the city of Jerusalem was rebuilt, was to appoint singers:

Now it came to pass, when the wall was built, and
I had set up the doors, and the porters and the
SINGERS . . . were appointed (Neh. 7:1).

62

Nehemiah knew the importance of music, that it was part of the restoration of worship. The singers were a part of the ministry of the Church. They had an integral part to play in the restoration of worship. Nehemiah was aware of the place that music had in the Church and so he appointed them. He chose them and set them in their place:

> The whole congregation together was forty and two thousand three hundred and threescore, beside their manservants and their maidservants, of whom there were seven thousand three hundred thirty and seven and they had two hundred forty and five SINGING MEN and SINGING WOMEN (Neh. 7:66-67).

> Of the sons of Asaph, the SINGERS were over the business of the house of God, For it was the king's commandment concerning them, that a certain portion should be for the SINGERS, due for every day (Neh. 11:22b, 23).

The singers were part of the church ministry and were paid by the tithes of the congregation (Nehemiah 13:5). They devoted much of their time to worshipping God, writing, playing and ministering in music. They probably spent time arranging, practicing, and directing music for the temple worship.

There was another revival in Judah when Priest Jehoiada restored the ministry of worship in the house of the Lord. He also knew the importance of music in the church and began to appoint the offices of musicians and singers:

> Also Jehoiada appointed the offices of the house of the Lord by the hand of the priests the Levites, whom David had distributed in the house of the Lord, to offer the burnt offerings of the Lord, as it is written in the law of Moses, with rejoicing and with SINGING, as it was ordained by David (2 Chron. 23:18).

Jehoiada was careful to set up the worship only the way God commanded it to be in the Law of Moses, and ordained by David in his tabernacle. It was getting *back* to the Word of God, *back* to the truth that had been lost.

Notice that when Israel fell into idolatry, the first thing to go was the ministry of music. With idolatry and carnality comes depression and joy is lost. The prophetic songs of God no longer flow out of a people. When this happens the anointing and presence of God disappears. One of the incidents in the history of Israel that points this out very clearly is when Moses was on Mount Sinai, and the children of Israel got tired of waiting for him. They became bored and restless. Together they asked Aaron to make a god for them, since they thought their God left them. They gathered all the gold and jewelry together, made a golden calf, and began to worship their idol. When Moses came down from the mountain with two tables of stone, all the people were dancing and singing around the calf of gold:

And when Joshua heard the noise of the people as they shouted, he said unto Moses, There is a noise of war in the camp. And he said, It is . . . the noise of them that SING do I hear (Exod. 32:17, 18).

The music they were singing and the songs that they were playing were so chaotic and confusing, that it sounded to Joshua like the torment and horror of war. Joshua never knew the music of Egypt, which is a type of the world or flesh, but Moses did. Joshua did not recognize the music Israel was making, but Moses, having come from Egypt, did. One of the very first things Israel lost when they fell into idolatry was the anointed ministry of music and the peace and harmony it brings.

Under Hezekiah, when God moved again in Israel, one of the first things to be restored was the song of the Lord and the anointing on the music. Hezekiah appointed the singers and the musicians just as Nehemiah did:

> And he [Hezekiah] set the Levites in the house of the Lord with CYMBALS, with PSALTERIES, and with HARPS, according to the commandment of David, and of Gad the king's seer, and Nathan the prophet: for so was the commandment of the Lord by his prophets (2 Chron. 29:25).

This verse clearly points out that God has commanded, through His prophets, that music is a ministry in the church and should be set up according to His pattern, which is found in the tabernacle of David.

Music is important to God:

> And the Levites stood with the INSTRUMENTS of David, and the priests with the TRUMPETS. And Hezekiah commanded to offer the burnt offering upon the altar. And when the burnt offering began, the SONG OF THE LORD began also with the TRUMPETS, and with the INSTRUMENTS ordained by David king of Israel. And all the congregation worshipped, and the SINGERS SANG, and the TRUMPETERS SOUNDED (2 Chron. 29:26-28a).

Hezekiah, like David, had a heart for worship. He knew the law of Moses and the commandments of David and the prophecies of Nathan the prophet. He knew how to set God's house in order. That is what is called Revival. Music is an evidence of a rebirth in God's people. When they receive again a revelation of truth, they will experience again a joyous sound. You show me a church that loves to sing and I'll show you a church that is spiritually alive. You show me a person that can't find it within himself to sing and rejoice, and I'll show you someone who has nothing to sing about. You show me a musician that is bubbling over with joyful music and I'll show you a musician who has a fresh revelation of Jesus.

CHAPTER X

Music in Heaven

One of the most exciting revelations that ever came to me personally was when I discovered, for the first time, that there will be music in heaven. When I was a young boy I had always heard that one day when we die, if we have become born again, we would be translated into heaven, each one of us having wings and white robes. Our activities in heaven would consist of flying around from cloud to cloud playing a harp and trying to keep out of mischief. However, I soon learned that this was not entirely true.

Through reading and studying God's Word for myself I discovered that the redeemed of the Lord will have white robes and will be involved in musical worship to God. John saw this very clearly when God gave him a vision of what was going to happen in heaven:

> After this I beheld, and, lo, a great multitude, which no man could number, of all nations, and kindreds, and people, and tongues, stood before the throne, and before the Lamb, clothed with white robes, and palms in their hands; And cried with a loud voice, saying [or SINGING], Salvation to our God which sitteth upon the throne, and unto the Lamb (Rev. 7:9, 10).

These were those who accepted God's free gift of salvation

and they were from every race and culture in the world. God allowed John to see them in white robes signifying the righteousness they had received through Jesus Christ.

But John not only saw them, he also heard them singing with a loud voice while waving palms in their hands. Did you know that there will be another Palm Sunday when we get to heaven? We will actually be waving palms, as Israel did when Jesus went into Jerusalem riding a colt. Instead of throwing our coats down before the King we will be throwing ourselves down before the throne and worshipping Him forever.

What was so interesting to me (when I discovered that there will be music in heaven), was to find out that the music is not only vocal but instrumental as well. Not only will there be singing in heaven, but there will be instruments of music. In fact, everyone in heaven will be playing harps:

> And I saw as it were a sea of glass mingled with fire: and them that had gotten the victory over the beast, and over his image, and over his mark, and over the number of his name, stand on the sea of glass, having the HARPS of God. And they SING the SONG OF MOSES the servant of God, and the SONG OF THE LAMB, saying [singing], Great and marvellous are thy works, Lord God Almighty; just and true are thy ways, thou King of saints (Rev. 15:2, 3).

All the overcomers in heaven that had gotten victory over the beast (the antichrist system) and had not received the mark of the number of the beast, John saw playing harps. They were musicians. The Bible is also very careful to mention that these overcomers were singers. In fact, John mentioned two of the songs they were singing: the 'Song of Moses' and the 'Song of the Lamb.' Praise the Lord! Not just those musically inclined here on earth will be playing instruments and singing, but everyone that overcomes the world, the flesh and the devil will be singing also. I want to be an overcomer so I'm overcoming those little things in my life that try to defeat me so that some day I will have enough confidence and strength in Jesus to overcome the beast and anti-Christ. According to this scripture in Revelation 15, we aren't translated before the beast comes on the scene but we overcome it. Hallelujah.

There was also another group of people that John saw in heaven:

> And I heard a voice from heaven, as the voice of many waters, and as the voice of a great thunder . . .

Notice the tremendous volume of audible worship that John heard. He compared it to the roar of many waterfalls. He didn't have a jet plane in his day that could break the sound barrier, or atomic blasts to compare this volume to. He lived in a quieter age where he didn't have all the noise pollution we have today. He compared this worship to *great* thunder.

> . . . and I heard the voice of HARPERS harping with their HARPS: And they SUNG as it were a new song before the throne, and before the four beasts, and the elders: and no man could learn that song but the hundred and forty and four thousand, which were redeemed from the earth (Rev. 14: 2, 3).

This group of 144,000, whoever they will be, will also be musicians and play harps. They also will be singing, but the Bible says that it will be a new song. As a songwriter this excites me. We will be singing in the Spirit a new song before the throne, making up the lyrics and the melody as we are inspired by the presence of Almighty God. There have been many times in church, as I've stood with my hands raised worshipping God, that I have received a new song from the Lord. When the opportunity comes in the service and I've received a quickening from God I begin to sing it out loud for the edification and comfort of the rest of the body.

Those are very special and precious moments when God moves that way by His Spirit.

God mentions the playing of instruments in heaven a third time in the book of Revelation. Three is a spiritually perfect number. It is exciting to know that God mentioned music three times in the vision to John, showing us that music is part of the perfect worship in heaven. Musician, take heart. God considers your talents and abilities important enough to be included as one of the forms of worship in heaven. Shy and timid singer, stand up tall and rejoice with a loud voice for God has chosen your ministry to be used in worship before the throne of the Lamb forever and ever:

> And when he [the Lamb] had taken the book, the four beasts and four and twenty elders fell down before the Lamb, having every one of them HARPS, and golden vials full of odours, which are the prayers of saints. And they SUNG a new SONG, saying, Thou art worthy to take the book, and to open the seals thereof: for thou wast slain, and hast redeemed us to God by thy blood out of every kindred, and tongue, and people, and nation; And hast made us unto our God kings and priests: and we shall reign on the earth (Rev. 5:8-10).

Everyone of the four beasts and twenty-four elders had harps. They were musicians along with the 144,000 and all the overcomers. What an orchestra! And the choir was just as large because the four beasts and twenty-four elders also sang a new song. The Bible records the lyrics of that song along with the song the angels sing and the song all creation sings:

> And I beheld, and I heard the voice of many angels round about the throne and the beasts and the elders: and the number of them was ten thousand times ten thousand, and thousands of thousands; Saying [singing] with a loud voice, Worthy is the

Lamb that was slain to receive power, and riches, and wisdom, and strength, and honour, and glory, and blessing (Rev. 5:11, 12).

I can hear that great multitude of over 102 million, singing right on pitch! What an angelic choir! What sweet orchestration. What a blend of musical instruments and voices. No wonder John said it sounded like, not ordinary thunder, but GREAT thunder.

I have been in services of about thirty thousand people with their hands raised worshipping the Lord out loud with their voices lifted up in praise. And there was a tremendous roar in that auditorium. Can you imagine the awesome praise that will ascend to God from a multitude of over 102 million before the throne, not to mention the animals.

And every creature which is in heaven, and on the earth, and under the earth, and such as are in the sea, and all that are in them, heard I [John] saying [singing], Blessing, and honour, and glory, and power be unto him that sitteth upon the throne, and unto the Lamb forever and ever (Rev. 5:13).

This may upset many people's theology to think animals praise the Lord. But the Word of God is truth and our ideas are wrong if they don't match up to God's Word. And the Bible clearly states:

And EVERY CREATURE which is in heaven, and [every creature which is] on the earth, and [every creature which is] under the earth, and such as are in the sea, and all THAT ARE IN THEM, heard I saying . . . (Rev. 5:13a).

That includes the birds, the deer, the earthworms, and the whales. It includes all that are in the heavens, on the earth, under the earth and in the sea. Even creation will be singing praise to God. Even creation is involved in the powerful ministry of music:

71

And the four beasts said, Amen. And the four and
twenty elders fell down and worshipped him that
liveth forever and ever (Rev. 5:14).

Everything will end in worship to Jesus. There is nothing that
will follow this scene in heaven, except an eternity of more
worship and praise to the One we love and we will all be part
of it.

In the first chapter of this book we discovered that
Lucifer fell from heaven because of his rebellion and pride.
When he fell his ministry of music also fell with him, leaving
a music minister's vacancy in heaven. No longer is there
someone who will lead the angelic hosts in worship to God
the Father. Who will be the anointed cherub that will cover
the throne of God, or will anyone? The Church is going to
fill that vacancy left by Lucifer. We, the redeemed of the
Lord, are going to lead all the angels, seraphim and cherubim,
and all of creation, in worship to God, with singing and playing on the harps. We, the bride of Christ, are going to stand
before the throne reunited with our beloved, singing love
songs for eternity; telling Him how much we love Him;
singing of His majesty and beauty. With our musical instruments we will accompany the angelic choirs as they sing "the
song of Moses" and the "Song of the Lamb." With clear and
perfect tone and pitch, our voices will tell of His great salvation and laud Him in the heavenlies. All the universe will
once again ring with harmonious music, as it did in the
beginning:

When the morning stars sang together, and all the
sons of God shouted for joy (Job 38:7).

The ministry of music is a beautiful and powerful one.
God has seen fit that it be present in the beginning, and that
it be restored once again to end all things. The accounts
in the Old and New Testaments of the ministry of music are
numerous. There are many scriptures that give us insight as
to what God requires in the music ministry. I challenge you,

as a musician, singer, songwriter, or arranger, to thoroughly examine the Word of God regarding your ministry. If you have been called of God to minister in music, find out what God expects of you and what responsibilities are placed on you as a priest (or minister) in God's house.

God has given you that talent and ability not to sit on a shelf and perish, but to flourish as you magnify and bless the Lord. God has given you that musical talent to worship Him. Pick up that violin or trombone that you haven't played for a while and dust it off and use it to praise the Lord! Take the musical instrument that God has given you and discipline yourself to practice, so that you can excel on it. God has commanded us to play skillfully with a loud noise. He wants us to play to the very best of our ability. Give yourself to your music. It is a ministry, not just entertainment, or accompaniment, in a service. It is not a preliminary to the sermon. It is an integral part of each service, divinely appointed by God as a ministry, or service, of praise unto Him. Take your music seriously. God has called you as a priest to minister before Him. For throughout eternity we are going to praise the Lord with loud singing and joyful worship on our instruments.

> All Hail King Jesus
> All Hail Emmanuel
> King of Kings, Lord of Lords
> Bright Morning Star
> And through all eternity
> I'm going to praise Him
> And for evermore
> I will reign with Him.
> —Dave Moody

A LIST OF SCRIPTURES ABOUT MUSIC IN THE BIBLE (839)

Instruments of Music

1. **Bells:**
   Exodus 28:33, 34
   Exodus 39:25, 26
   Zechariah 14:20

2. **Brass:**
   1 Corinthians 13:1

3. **Cornets:**
   2 Samuel 6:5
   1 Chronicles 15:28
   2 Chronicles 15:14
   Psalms 98:6
   Daniel 3:5, 7, 10, 15
   Hosea 5:8

4. **Cymbals:**
   2 Samuel 6:5
   1 Chronicles 13:8
   1 Chronicles 15:16, 19, 28
   1 Chronicles 16:5, 42
   1 Chronicles 25:1, 6
   2 Chronicles 5:12, 13
   2 Chronicles 29:25
   Ezra 3:10
   Nehemiah 12:27
   Psalms 150:5
   1 Corinthians 13:1

5. **Dulcimer (a bagpipe):**
   Daniel 3:5, 10, 15

6. **Flute:**
   Daniel 3:5, 7, 10, 15

7. **Harps:**
   Genesis 4:21
   Genesis 31:27
   1 Samuel 10:5
   1 Samuel 16:16, 23
   2 Samuel 6:5
   1 Kings 10:12
   1 Chronicles 13:8
   1 Chronicles 15:16, 21, 28
   1 Chronicles 16:5
   1 Chronicles 25:1, 3, 6
   2 Chronicles 5:12, 15
   2 Chronicles 9:11
   2 Chronicles 20:28
   2 Chronicles 29:25
   Nehemiah 12:27
   Job 21:12
   Job 30:31
   Psalms 33:2
   Psalms 43:4
   Psalms 49:4
   Psalms 57:8
   Psalms 71:22
   Psalms 81:2
   Psalms 92:3
   Psalms 98:5 (twice)
   Psalms 108:2
   Psalms 137:2
   Psalms 147:7
   Psalms 149:3
   Psalms 150:3
   Isaiah 5:12
   Isaiah 16:11
   Isaiah 23:16
   Isaiah 24:8

Harps (continued):
Isaiah 30:32
Ezekiel 26:13
Daniel 3:5, 7, 10, 15
1 Corinthians 14:7 (twice)
Revelation 5:8
Revelation 14:2 (twice)
Revelation 15:2
Revelation 18:22

8. Organ:
Genesis 4:21
Job 21:12
Job 30:31
Psalms 150:4

9. Pipes:
1 Samuel 10:5
1 Kings 1:40
Isaiah 5:12
Isaiah 30:29
Jeremiah 48:36
Ezekiel 28:13
Zechariah 4:2
Zechariah 4:12
Matthew 11:17
Luke 7:32
1 Corinthians 14:7

10. Psaltery:
1 Samuel 10:5
2 Samuel 6:5
1 Kings 10:12
1 Chronicles 13:8
1 Chronicles 15:16, 20, 28
1 Chronicles 16:5
1 Chronicles 26:1, 6
2 Chronicles 5:12

Psaltery (continued):
2 Chronicles 9:11
2 Chronicles 20:28
2 Chronicles 29:25
Nehemiah 12:27
Psalms 33:2
Psalms 57:8
Psalms 71:22
Psalms 81:2
Psalms 92:3
Psalms 108:2
Psalms 144:9
Psalms 150:3
Daniel 3:5, 7, 10, 15

11. **Ram's Horns:**
Joshua 6:4, 5, 6, 8, 13

12. **Sackbut (a wind instrument):**
Daniel 3:5, 7, 10, 15

13. **Sheminith (8-stringed lyre):**
(octave, deep voices)
1 Chronicles 15:21
Psalms 6
Psalms 12

14. **Tabret(s) (tambourines):**
Genesis 31:27
1 Samuel 10:5
1 Samuel 18:6
Job 17:6
Isaiah 5:12
Isaiah 24:8
Isaiah 30:32
Jeremiah 31:4
Ezekiel 28:13

15. Timbrels (tambourines):
  Exodus 15:20
  Job 21:12
  Judges 11:34
  2 Samuel 6:5
  1 Chronicles 13:8
  Psalms 68:25
  Psalms 81:2
  Psalms 149:3
  Psalms 150:4

16. Trumpets:
  Exodus 19:13, 16, 19
  Exodus 20:18
  Leviticus 23:24
  Leviticus 25:9
  Numbers 10:2, 4, 8, 9, 10
  Numbers 29:1
  Numbers 31:6
  Joshua 6:4, 5, 6, 8, 9, 13, 16, 20
  Judges 3:27
  Judges 6:34
  Judges 7:8, 16, 18, 19, 20, 22
  1 Samuel 13:3
  2 Samuel 2:28
  2 Samuel 6:15
  2 Samuel 15:10
  2 Samuel 18:16
  2 Samuel 20:1, 22
  1 Kings 1:34, 39, 41
  2 Kings 9:13
  2 Kings 11:14
  2 Kings 12:13
  1 Chronicles 13:8
  1 Chronicles 15:24, 28
  1 Chronicles 16:6, 42
  2 Chronicles 5:12, 13
  2 Chronicles 7:6

Trumpets (continued):
2 Chronicles 13:12, 14
2 Chronicles 15:14
2 Chronicles 20:28
2 Chronicles 23:13
2 Chronicles 29:26, 27, 28
Ezra 3:10
Nehemiah 4:18, 20
Nehemiah 12:35, 41
Job 39:24, 25
Psalms 47:5
Psalms 81:3
Psalms 98:6
Psalms 150:3
Isaiah 18:3
Isaiah 27:13
Isaiah 58:1
Jeremiah 4:5, 19, 21
Jeremiah 6:1, 17
Jeremiah 42:14
Jeremiah 51:27
Ezekiel 7:14
Ezekiel 33:3, 4, 5, 6
Hosea 5:8
Hosea 8:1
Joel 2:1, 15
Amos 2:2
Amos 3:6
Zephaniah 1:16
Zechariah 9:14
Matthew 6:2
Matthew 24:31
1 Corinthians 14:8
1 Corinthians 15:52
1 Thessalonians 4:16
Hebrews 12:19
Revelation 1:10
Revelation 4:1

Trumpets (continued):
   Revelation 8:2, 6, 13
   Revelation 9:14
   Revelation 18:22

21. Viols:
   Isaiah 5:12
   Isaiah 14:11
   Amos 5:23
   Amos 6:5

* * *

Musical Terms, etc.

1. **Alamoth—soprano female voices:**
   1 Chronicles 15:20
   Psalm 46

2. **Altascheth—"destroy not"— maybe opening lyrics of popular song:**
   Psalms 57
   Psalms 58
   Psalms 59
   Psalms 75

3. **Clap:**
   2 Kings 11:12
   Psalms 47:1
   Psalms 98:8
   Isaiah 55:12
   Ezekiel 25:6

4. **Dance, Dances or Dancing:**
   Exodus 15:20
   Exodus 32:19

Dance, Dances or Dancing cont'd):
Judges 11:34
Judges 21:21, 23
1 Samuel 18:6
1 Samuel 21:11
1 Samuel 29:5
1 Samuel 30:16
2 Samuel 6:14, 16
1 Chronicles 15:29
Job 21:11
Psalms 30:11
Psalms 149:3
Psalms 150:4
Ecclesiastes 3:4
Isaiah 13:21
Jeremiah 31:4, 13
Lamentations 5:15
Matthew 11:17
Matthew 14:6
Mark 6:22
Luke 7:32
Luke 15:25

5. **Gittith (harmony):**
Psalms 8
Psalms 81
Psalms 84

6. **Jonathelemrechokim:**
Psalms 56

7. **Leannoth (sing loudly to create attention):**
Psalms 88

8. **Mahalath (title or word of a popular song):**
Psalms 53
Psalms 88

9. **Maschil:**
   Psalms 32
   Psalms 42
   Psalms 44
   Psalms 45
   Psalms 52
   Psalms 53
   Psalms 54
   Psalms 55
   Psalms 74
   Psalms 78
   Psalms 88
   Psalms 89
   Psalms 142

10. **Melody:**
    Isaiah 23:16
    Isaiah 51:3
    Amos 5:23
    Ephesians 5:19

11. **Michtam (a poem, possibly a lyric):**
    Psalms 16
    Psalms 56
    Psalms 57
    Psalms 58
    Psalms 59
    Psalms 60

12. **Minstrels (players of stringed instruments):**
    2 Kings 3:15 (twice)
    Matthew 9:23

13. **Music, Musical, Musicians:**
    1 Samuel 18:6
    1 Chronicles 15:16
    1 Chronicles 16:42
    2 Chronicles 5:13

13. Music, Musical, Musicians (cont'd):

2 Chronicles 7:6
2 Chronicles 23:13
2 Chronicles 34:12
Nehemiah 12:36
Psalms 4
Psalms 5
Psalms 6
Psalms 8
Psalms 9
Psalms 11
Psalms 12
Psalms 13
Psalms 14
Psalms 18
Psalms 19
Psalms 20
Psalms 21
Psalms 22
Psalms 31
Psalms 36
Psalms 39
Psalms 40
Psalms 41
Psalms 42
Psalms 44
Psalms 45
Psalms 46
Psalms 47
Psalms 49
Psalms 51
Psalms 52
Psalms 53
Psalms 54
Psalms 55
Psalms 56
Psalms 57
Psalms 58

13. Music, Musical, Musicians (cont'd):

Psalms 59
Psalms 60
Psalms 61
Psalms 62
Psalms 64
Psalms 65
Psalms 66
Psalms 67
Psalms 68
Psalms 69
Psalms 70
Psalms 75
Psalms 76
Psalms 77
Psalms 80
Psalms 81
Psalms 84
Psalms 85
Psalms 88
Psalms 109
Psalms 139
Psalms 140
Ecclesiastes 2:8
Ecclesiastes 12:4
Lamentations 3:63
Lamentations 5:14
Daniel 3:5, 7, 10, 15
Daniel 6:18
Amos 6:5
Luke 15:25
Revelation 18:22

14. Muthlabben, "die for the son" (title of a popular song):

Psalms 9

15. Neginah, or Neginoth (stringed instrument):
Psalms 4
Psalms 6
Psalms 54
Psalms 55
Psalms 61
Psalms 67
Psalms 76

16. Nehiloth (flute):
Psalms 5

17. Pipers:
Revelation 18:22

18. Played:
1 Samuel 18:7

19. Players (of musical instruments):
1 Samuel 16:16, 17, 18, 23
1 Samuel 18:10
1 Samuel 19:9
2 Kings 3:15
1 Chronicles 15:29
Psalms 33:3
Psalms 68:25
Ezekiel 33:32

20. Psalms, Psalmist:
2 Samuel 23:1
1 Chronicles 16:7, 9
Psalms 3
Psalms 4
Psalms 5
Psalms 6
Psalms 8
Psalms 9
Psalms 11

Psalms, Psalmist (continued):

Psalms 12
Psalms 13
Psalms 14
Psalms 15
Psalms 18
Psalms 19
Psalms 20
Psalms 21
Psalms 22
Psalms 23
Psalms 24
Psalms 25
Psalms 26
Psalms 27
Psalms 28
Psalms 29
Psalms 30
Psalms 31
Psalms 32
Psalms 34
Psalms 35
Psalms 36
Psalms 37
Psalms 38
Psalms 39
Psalms 40
Psalms 41
Psalms 47
Psalms 48
Psalms 49
Psalms 50
Psalms 51
Psalms 52
Psalms 53
Psalms 54
Psalms 55
Psalms 61

Psalms, Psalmist (continued):

Psalms 62
Psalms 63
Psalms 64
Psalms 65
Psalms 66
Psalms 67
Psalms 68
Psalms 69
Psalms 70
Psalms 72
Psalms 73
Psalms 75
Psalms 76
Psalms 77
Psalms 79
Psalms 80
Psalms 81
Psalms 81:2
Psalms 82
Psalms 83
Psalms 84
Psalms 85
Psalms 87
Psalms 88
Psalms 92
Psalms 95:2
Psalms 98
Psalms 98:5
Psalms 100
Psalms 101
Psalms 103
Psalms 105:2
Psalms 108
Psalms 109
Psalms 110
Psalms 138
Psalms 139

Psalms, Psalmist (continued):
Psalms 140
Psalms 141
Psalms 143
Psalms 144
Psalms 145
Luke 20:42
Luke 24:44
Acts 1:20
Acts 13:33, 35
Ephesians 5:19
Colossians 3:16
James 5:13

21. Sang, Sing, Singer(s), Singing, Song(s), Sung:
Genesis 31:27
Exodus 15:1, 21
Exodus 32:18
Numbers 21:17
Judges 5:1, 3
1 Samuel 18:6
1 Samuel 21:11
1 Samuel 29:5
2 Samuel 19:35
2 Samuel 22:50
1 Kings 4:32
1 Kings 10:12
1 Chronicles 6:32, 33
1 Chronicles 9:33
1 Chronicles 13:8
1 Chronicles 15:16, 19, 27
1 Chronicles 16:9, 23, 33
1 Chronicles 23:5
1 Chronicles 25:7
2 Chronicles 5:12, 13
2 Chronicles 9:11
2 Chronicles 20:21, 22

Sang, Sing, Singer(s), Singing,
Song(s), Sung (continued):
   2 Chronicles 23:13, 18
   2 Chronicles 29:28, 30
   2 Chronicles 30:21
   2 Chronicles 35:15, 25
   Ezra 2:41, 65, 70
   Ezra 3:11
   Ezra 7:7, 24
   Ezra 10:24
   Nehemiah 7:1, 44, 67,73
   Nehemiah 10:28, 39
   Nehemiah 11:22, 23
   Nehemiah 12:27, 28, 29, 42, 45, 46, 47
   Nehemiah 13:5, 10
   Job 29:13
   Job 35:10
   Job 38:7
   Psalms 7
   Psalms 7:17
   Psalms 9:2, 11
   Psalms 13:6
   Psalms 18:49
   Psalms 21:13
   Psalms 27:6
   Psalms 28:7
   Psalms 30:4, 12
   Psalms 32:7
   Psalms 33:2, 3
   Psalms 40:3
   Psalms 42:8
   Psalms 45:1
   Psalms 46:1
   Psalms 47:6, 7
   Psalms 48:1
   Psalms 51:14
   Psalms 57:7, 9
   Psalms 59:16, 17

Sang, Sing, Singer(s), Singing, Song(s), Sung (continued):

Psalms 61:8
Psalms 65:13
Psalms 66:2, 4
Psalms 67:4
Psalms 68:4, 25, 32
Psalms 69:12, 30
Psalms 71:22, 23
Psalms 75:9
Psalms 76:1
Psalms 77:6
Psalms 81:1
Psalms 83:1
Psalms 87:7
Psalms 88:1
Psalms 89:1, 17
Psalms 92:1
Psalms 95:1
Psalms 96:1, 2
Psalms 98:1, 4, 5
Psalms 100:2
Psalms 101:1
Psalms 104:12, 33
Psalms 105:2, 3
Psalms 106:12
Psalms 108:1, 3
Psalms 118:14
Psalms 119:54
Psalms 120:1
Psalms 121:1
Psalms 122:1
Psalms 123:1
Psalms 124:1
Psalms 125:1
Psalms 126:1, 2
Psalms 127:1
Psalms 128:1

Sang, Sing, Singer(s), Singing, Song(s), Sung (continued):
Psalms 129:1
Psalms 130:1
Psalms 131:1
Psalms 132:1
Psalms 133:1
Psalms 134:1
Psalms 135:3
Psalms 137:3, 4
Psalms 138:1, 5
Psalms 144:9
Psalms 145:7
Psalms 146:2
Psalms 147:1, 7
Psalms 149:1, 3, 5
Proverbs 25:20
Proverbs 29:6
Song of Solomon 1:1
Song of Solomon 2:12
Ecclesiastes 2:8
Ecclesiastes 7:5
Isaiah 5:1
Isaiah 12:2, 5
Isaiah 14:7
Isaiah 16:10
Isaiah 23:15, 16
Isaiah 24:9, 14, 16
Isaiah 26:1, 19
Isaiah 27:2
Isaiah 30:29
Isaiah 35:10, 26
Isaiah 38.20
Isaiah 42:10, 11
Isaiah 44:23
Isaiah 48:20
Isaiah 49:13
Isaiah 51:11

Sang, Sing, Singer(s), Singing,
Song(s), Sung (continued):
  Isaiah 52:8, 9
  Isaiah 54:1
  Isaiah 55:12
  Isaiah 65:14
  Jeremiah 20:13
  Jeremiah 31:7, 12
  Jeremiah 51:48
  Lamentations 3:14
  Ezekiel 26:13
  Ezekiel 27:25, 66
  Ezekiel 33:32
  Ezekiel 40:44
  Daniel 3:27
  Hosea 2:15
  Amos 5:23
  Amos 8:3, 10
  Habakkuk 3:19
  Zephaniah 2:14
  Zephaniah 3:14, 17
  Zechariah 2:10
  Matthew 26:30
  Mark 14:26
  Acts 16:25
  Romans 15:19
  1 Corinthians 14:15
  Ephesians 5:19
  Colossians 3:16
  Hebrews 2:12
  James 5:13
  Revelation 5:9
  Revelation 14:3
  Revelation 15:3

22. Selah (vocal pause, change instrumenta-
    tion, modulate, or musical interlude):
    Joshua 15:38

Selah (continued):
2 Kings 14:7
Psalms 3:2, 4, 8
Psalms 4:2, 4
Psalms 7:5
Psalms 9:16, 20
Psalms 20:3
Psalms 21:2
Psalms 24:6, 10
Psalms 32:4, 5, 7
Psalms 39:5, 11
Psalms 44:8
Psalms 46:3, 7
Psalms 47:4
Psalms 48:8
Psalms 49:13, 15
Psalms 50:6
Psalms 52:3, 5
Psalms 54:3
Psalms 55:7, 19
Psalms 57:3, 6
Psalms 59:5, 13
Psalms 60:4
Psalms 61:4
Psalms 62:4, 8
Psalms 66:4, 7, 15
Psalms 67:1, 4
Psalms 68:7, 19, 32
Psalms 75:3
Psalms 76:3, 9
Psalms 77:3, 9, 15
Psalms 81:7
Psalms 82:2
Psalms 83:8
Psalms 84:4, 8
Psalms 85:2
Psalms 87 3, 6
Psalms 88:7, 10

Selah (continued):
Psalms 89:4, 37, 45, 48
Psalms 140:3, 5, 8
Psalms 143:6
Isaiah 16:1
Habakkuk 3:3, 9, 13

23. **Shiggaion, Shigionoth (various songs or rambling lyric):**
Psalms 7
Habakkuk 3:1

24. **Shoshannim or Shoshannimeduth (a musical term):**
Psalms 45
Psalms 69
Psalms 80

25. **Shushaneduth (a musical term):**
Psalms 60

Music seminars and workshops by the author are available upon request. Other books, sermon tapes, and recordings are available by writing:

LaMar Boschman Ministries
c/o Revival Press
P.O. Box 130
Bedford, TX 76021